CLAY
❈ IN ❈
GOD'S
HANDS

D. R. Fogle

ISBN 978-1-63885-247-6 (Paperback)
ISBN 978-1-63885-248-3 (Digital)

Meyer, J. (2006). *The Everyday Life Bible. Amplified Version* (1st ed.). New York, NY: Warner Faith.

Covenant Books
11661 Hwy 707
Murrells Inlet, SC 29576
www.covenantbooks.com

Illustrations by Lisa D. Galentine

DEDICATION

To my Lord who directed me and blessed my reasons for sharing these words of redemption and His love. May my family and all who read this have hope and understand God's forgiveness and grace in our lives.

To my wife and soul mate of forty-five years—thank you, Lisa, for your patience and help in writing down these words. Thank you for your care in my days of need. My love and gratitude are eternal—thank you for everything.

And to my children and grandchildren whose love first gave me the will to live and finish this short work in hopes of saving their souls so that we may spend eternity in the Lord's kingdom.

Thanks to Mary Ann for helping me organize and edit my stories. May the master artist, our Lord in heaven, bless her for her work.

May the God of our eternal souls bless all those who helped me finish this work before I pass into His clay covered hands and fulfill His plans for my next journey.

My love to all.

Science tells us we need at least four basic elements to survive: water, air, food, and light. Look at what Jesus says about Himself in the Bible:

I am the living water.
I am the breath of life.
I am the bread of life.
I am the light of the world.
Science is right: we need Jesus to live!

(Source: Phil Fischer—Devotional Four Basic Elements)

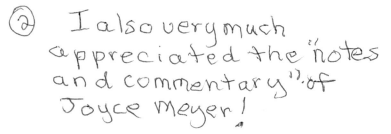

② I also very much appreciated the "notes and commentary" of Joyce Meyer!

CONTENTS

FOREWORD

As a child, and throughout my life, I remember my father, a wise gentle man, telling me that every person we meet has a story to tell, and taking time to genuinely listen to those stories makes each of us better people. I have reflected on and tried to follow this wisdom, and in return, I have been blessed.

Denny's wife, Lisa, and I worked together, shared our stories, and became friends. Through this friendship I learned about Lisa's husband, Denny, and his journey of faith as he battled cancer. My husband, a man of deep faith, had also valiantly battled cancer.

Lisa told me that Denny was keeping a journal to share with his family. She asked if I would consider reading and editing this journal. I was honored to be asked. I read and returned the journal without a single edit because Denny's story, told in his words, was such a powerful testament to his faith in God and his love of family that to make changes just felt wrong.

Denny and I finally met. He shared that he had not only journaled but had also written a book of stories about his life to document and help his family and others to understand his journey of faith, his battle with cancer, and God's unending love throughout. He asked me to read the stories and smooth out any rough spots.

Reading Denny's journal and stories, I have been deeply moved by his unshakable faith in God and his willingness to share that faith with the family he so dearly loves and with those whose lives he touches. What I genuinely appreciate is Denny's openness in sharing his personal struggles and battles in his day-by-day commitment to be a man of God and to lead a good and holy life. His fierce love of God and family and amazing courage in battling cancer is a powerful story. My father would agree that I am a better person for having met Denny and listened to his story. Thank you, Denny.

PREFACE

Have you ever had an incident in your life that just can't be explained? Many people with good memories can recall such times. I believe these so-called close calls are more than just good luck. I firmly believe they are acts of God and His angels interceding by protecting us because He has not finished His plans for our lives; He has not yet completed the masterpiece we are destined to become.

As an example, my wife was sitting in her car in a parking lot when a full-size pickup truck smashed into the driver-side door. The truck completely totaled her small car, and the fire department had to use the jaws of life to remove her from the vehicle. She survived with no major injuries.

My wife told me later that, at the moment of impact, she felt a hand pushing her toward the passenger side of her car. Good luck? I think not. The master artist had her in His hands knowing that, in the future, she was going to take very good care of me when my health failed. And He had many more plans for her, with a final goal of eternal bliss in heaven.

I, for one, do not believe in good luck. I have learned that every moment and incident is our Lord molding our lives with His plans for us during our earthly trials, and ultimately, the eternal life we are to have with Him, our Lord and Savior. All praise and thanks to our maker, the ultimate master artist.

Some, when reading these stories about my experiences, will think I'm a radical living a make-believe life. I assure you, every event on these pages is true, accurate, and honest. As you will find out, my whole life, with all these stories and events, has been God molding my future. And when the time was right, He led me to write them all down with the purpose of saving souls even if it is just one or two.

After sixty years, every dream and every event is as clear in my mind as if it took place yesterday. Any rewards from the hours of telling my life stories will come when I greet the soul, or souls, at the gates of heaven where I will welcome them home.

My goal is to let you know that through trials and adversity, valuable lessons can be learned. God's powerful and creative hands are on every moment of our lives. He is molding and forming us into the worthy souls with whom He wants to spend eternity.

If we believe and trust in Him, He will do wonderous acts with our lives so that we can enjoy His eternal grace and love. I have found that all my trials and hard times have had purpose and have brought me back to a more perfect faith and relationship with God.

One of the most profound lessons I've learned in my years of life's trials is that love is the only thing that matters—love of God, love of family, and love of our fellow man. If you study the life of Jesus, you'll find He is love and, through His teachings, He shows us how to follow Him in love.

We must let go of the heavy burdens of grudges, hate, and unforgiveness by turning them over to Jesus. He even promised to lighten our loads and carry them for us. But even harder than that, we must learn to forgive ourselves. Our Savior has already done that through His sacrifice on the cross.

All we have to do is believe and tell the Lord that we are sorry for our sins. At that moment, He will reside in us by his Holy Spirit and start to prepare us by molding our lives to be with Him forever.

Often, after living through an event that should have taken me, I would wonder why I was spared and allowed to live. It has taken me over sixty years to find out just what His plans are. It came to me that revealing my testimonies found in these pages was His goal. Through most of these events, God knew I wasn't ready, and until I was ready, He wouldn't take me. So He molded and formed me into a person who is now ready and who understands that He wants me to pass this knowledge on to others.

I'm not a special human, just one who, from a very early age, had faith in our Redeemer Jesus Christ. Even in the bad times I would turn to Him for help, and He always carried me. I would tell Jesus, "Without You, I am nothing." I never got mad at Him and always leaned on Him. I can't even imagine how nonbelievers deal with the rocky road we travel in this short and trying life we live.

Some would say I must be a little off my rocker to praise and thank a God who would make me suffer the way I have from an early age: asthma until the age of twelve, a blood disease in the third grade, overweight and teased every day at school, beaten up so badly in high school that I couldn't go to my graduation, abuse by a beating from my sixth-grade nun, a motorcycle wreck my senior year. I could continue, but these were all just bumps bringing me even closer to God.

I hope you understand and see how everything we go through has a reason. It's not just the trials we have to endure, but the lessons we must learn from our adversities—all to enjoy eternity with our Creator in heaven.

There is truth in the old saying that what doesn't kill you makes you stronger. I hope you will learn this from my stories, revelations, and even miracles. Turn yourselves over to God and become the clay in His hands. Let Him form you into a masterpiece, ready to walk with Him for an eternity of peace, love, and joy with no more suffering, sickness, or trials ever again. Praise and thanks to our almighty God.

Read now the wonders, miracles, and signs of my faith journey with the Master Artist we have in heaven.

Scriptures

Has the potter no right over the clay, to make out of the same mass (lump) one vessel for beauty *and* distinction *and* honorable use, and another for menial *or* ignoble *and* dishonorable use? (Romans 9:21, The Everyday Life Bible Amplified Version Featuring Notes and Commentary by Joyce Meyer)

A man's mind plans his way, but the Lord directs his steps *and* makes them sure. (Proverbs 16:9)

15

The Lord is my Rock, my
Fortress, and my Deliverer; my
God, my keen *and* firm Strength
in Whom I will trust *and* take
refuge, my Shield, and the Horn
of my salvation, my High Tower.
(Psalm 18:2)

He drew me up out of a
horrible pit [a pit of tulmult and
of destruction], out of the miry
clay (froth and slime), and set my
feet upon a rock, steadying my
steps *and* establishing my goings.
(Psalm 40:2)

LESSONS OF MY YOUTH

The Scotty Dream

The memory of this early dream is so vivid that it will stay in my mind the rest of my life, etched into my brain by seeing it over and over again. It was an early message from God that the way to life eternal with our Father in heaven is not always the easiest and most inviting path to travel. This dream was the beginning of the Lord molding me in a lifelong journey of His love and grace. Thank you to the holiest of Holy for picking up this lump of clay and choosing me to become a masterpiece in the late winter of my life.

When young, seven or eight years old, I would experience this dream many times and it was always the same. I was walking down a beautiful and peaceful street when I spotted a cozy stone bungalow with the cutest Scotty dog sitting on the front stoop. The house and dog were so inviting, and I couldn't resist going up to the little dog. Behind it was the front door, which I had to open. Directly inside were steps that led me straight down to a fiery inferno. The basement looked like hell itself. I could hear screams and moaning. I would pull the door shut and run up the street.

At this point, everything would become very peaceful and the dream would end. I had some deep thoughts about this dream, and I could only think the Lord was telling me that beautiful and earthly things would not be getting me access to heaven.

Even at my advanced age, this dream is as sharp as it was over sixty years ago. My life's lessons began at a very early age. Praise God for His love and teaching.

Scriptures

Keep on asking and it will be given you; keep on seeking and you will find; keep on knocking [reverently] and [the door] will be opened to you. (Matthew 7:7)

Then You scare me with dreams and terrify me through visions. (Job 7:14)

Lord, I love the habitation of Your house, and the place where Your glory dwells. (Psalm 26:8)

Drag me not away with the wicked, with the workers of iniquity, who speak peace with their neighbors, but malice *and* mischief are in their hearts. (Psalm 28:3)

The Stolen Race Car

This story is as fresh in my mind as the day it took place. God showed me a visible sign of his love and forgiveness. The memory starts with sin and turns into a revelation of God's spirit active in my life. At the age of nine, I was blessed with the knowledge of sin and redemption and His love. All thanks to my parents for the teaching I was receiving in school, and above all, thanks to my precious Lord in heaven. How blessed can a young boy be to find all this at such an early age? Blessed be the Lord and all His miracles.

My day began with playing with a neighbor boy whose family had traveled to Europe several times. He had a small toy race car made of metal which was unlike any toy I had ever seen. The car was painted and had steerable front wheels, rubber tires, and chrome spinners on all the wheels. The hood raised to show the engine, and it was very detailed. I wanted that car badly.

My friend's mother called him inside. I snatched up the car and took it home. I had never stolen anything, and I felt very uncomfortable with my actions. That night, I could not get to sleep. I cried, then I prayed, and then I prayed and cried some more. I asked the Lord to forgive me and promised Him I would return the car the next day.

I still could not sleep. I started crying again, and I prayed some more. Suddenly my bedroom lit up brightly. Standing at the end of my bed was a light shaped like Jesus or an angel with hands reaching out toward me. I remember there was not much detail— just a shape of light. I was filled with peace and calm, and soon fell asleep.

The next day, I went to my neighbor's house to return the toy, as I had promised in my prayers. I admitted stealing the car and told him how sorry I was for my actions. My friend insisted I keep the car. After telling him that a promise was made to God and I couldn't keep the car, he still refused to take it back. To this day I wonder where that little race car ended up.

The lesson I learned was that by confessing my wrongs, forgiveness could be earned. Some might say the vision in my room that night was a dream. But I can tell you, I was as awake as I am now writing this down. The sleep came afterward. This incident was my first revelation of the peace and love of our beloved Lord.

Scriptures

And suddenly an Angel of the Lord appeared [standing beside him] and a light shone in the place where he was. And the angel gently smote Peter on the side and awakened him, saying, Get up quickly! And the chains fell off his hands. (Acts 12:7)

Wash me thoroughly [and repeatedly] from my iniquity *and* guilt and cleanse me *and* make me wholly pure from my sin! (Psalm 51:2)

In Him we have redemption (deliverance and salvation) through His blood, the remission (forgiveness) of our offenses (shortcomings and trespasses), in accordance with the riches *and* the generosity of His gracious favor. (Ephesians 1:7)

The Angel of the Lord encamps around those who fear Him [who revere and worship Him with awe] and each of them He delivers. (Psalm 34:7)

He speaks, who heard the words of God and knew the knowledge of the Most High, who saw the vision of the Almighty, falling down, but having his eyes opened *and* uncovered. (Numbers 24:16)

Then does He Who supplies you with His marvelous [Holy] Spirit and works powerfully *and* miraculously among you do so on [the grounds of your doing] what the Law demands, or because of your believing in *and* adhering to *and* trusting in *and* relying on the message that you heard? (Galatians 3:5)

Are not the angels all ministering spirits (servants) sent out in the service [of God for the assistance] of those who are to inherit salvation? (Hebrews 1:14)

THE MIDDLE YEARS

Who Were They?

This is a story of guardian angels. I don't know if they were mine or my father's, but either way, I'm thankful for them showing up when they did. The appearance of these two young men could not be explained by me or my entire family who was present. Because of this mystery, I thought it was worthy of mention in my life's journey and unexplained happenings. The incident took place on a summer evening and remains fresh in my mind. I would have to say that what took place that evening probably helped change many lives. Praise the Lord and all His heavenly hosts.

A friend and I were having a burial ceremony in his backyard for one of our beloved parakeets when a drunk adult neighbor interrupted our ceremony and threatened to kick my butt all over the neighborhood. He said I had been picking on his kids. But it was his kids who were picking on me. Fearing for my well-being, I could do no more than agree not to bother his kids.

When I returned home, I told my father what the grown-up neighbor had said to me. My dad was furious, and he shouted over to the neighbor, "If you have something to say to my son, you better come talk to me first." The neighbor quickly headed over, and I thought to myself I had done the wrong thing by telling dad.

My parents were going out that evening and were all dressed up. The neighbor stopped on our property line and started with his drunken threats. My father pulled off his suitcoat and started toward the big-mouthed neighbor who was known to hit other neighbors and to carry knives. I was scared to death my dad was going to get hurt.

Then suddenly, a car stopped at the end of our driveway and two handsome young men, about twenty years old, came up the drive and each took one of my father's arms to stop his advancement. I remember them talking gently to my dad and telling him that fighting with this man wasn't worth it. Then, with stern voices, they told the neighbor to go home. I guess he wasn't so drunk that he didn't realize he was outnumbered, so he left.

The two strangers returned to their car and drove off. Nobody had ever before seen that car or the two men who stopped. How did they know what was about to happen? The houses were close together in our neighborhood, and the driveway is small. How could they possibly know what was happening? Who were these men who had never been seen before or after this incident?

Why do I remember this so vividly after half a century has passed? I sincerely believe they were either my guardian angels or my father's. It is the only thing that makes sense. I know how thankful I was and that I gave a prayer of thanks to our wonderful God and all His helpers.

Scriptures

For this [very] night there stood by my side an angel of the God to Whom I belong and Whom I serve *and* worship. (Acts 27:23)

God is our Refuge and Strength [mighty *and* impenetrable to temptation], a very present *and* well-proved help in trouble. (Psalm 46:1)

So too the [Holy] Spirit comes to our aid *and* bears us up in our weakness; for we do not know what prayer to offer *nor* how to offer it worthily as we ought, but the Spirit Himself goes to meet our supplication *and* pleads in our behalf with unspeakable yearnings *and* groanings too deep for utterance. (Romans 8:26)

The Lesson of Loss

New Year's Day in the twenty-sixth year of my life was a devastating and sad day. A call came from my mother who was at the hospital, and that's never good. She said simply that my brother had an accident at work. He didn't survive the 440-volt shock he received from an overhead crane at the factory where he worked. The news hit me like the electric shock that took my brother's life. I literally fell to my knees and screamed.

I had lost many loved ones and friends, but my brother was only four years older than me. We grew up together as friends. When he was with me, I knew the older neighbor kids would not pick on me. It was okay for him to give me a hard time, as brothers often do, but nobody else had that right.

I loved my brother and could not believe this was happening. The shock was numbing. At the time, it was the worst thing I had ever experienced. I just wanted to wake up from this horrible dream, but of course that didn't happen. All I could do was pray that he was in God's favor and write a eulogy to be read at his service.

My brother left behind a wonderful wife and three children—two sons and a daughter. The oldest son had to have hernia surgery when he was just a few months old. His little heart stopped during the procedure. It took over five minutes to resuscitate him which left him with severe brain damage.

My brother and his wife had their work cut out for them. They had over 150 volunteers come in during the week to help them. This was seven or eight volunteers moving his limbs, in a swimming motion on a large wooden table, just to keep his muscles alive so they wouldn't become too stiff. The work was from daylight to dark, and he was just eight years old when my brother passed.

The evening of my brother's accident, the family went to his house to gather and grieve. My father, who already had a list of health problems, became angry with God. He asked, "Why would God not take me instead of a young man who had to leave behind so much?" He started to make other angry statements to our Lord.

That's when I stopped him. I said, "Pop, we can never understand the will of God, but we can't become mad at His decisions. Perhaps someday we will understand." I told Pop that the Lord is all we have right now and we should accept the will of God and pray that his soul was with God and in a better place. This loss nearly tore the family apart, but we all got through it with help from our Lord.

Just months after this terrible time, I received another phone call from my mother. She was in tears and told me that my brother's oldest son aspirated and passed away during the night. Please forgive me, but I just couldn't cry for my nephew. It was at that moment, understanding filled my thoughts.

My nephew would never have a fulfilling life with any hope of normality. I could now picture him hand-in-hand with my brother in paradise—running, laughing, and talking. Our loving Father sent my nephew to heaven to be with his dad.

I hope this all makes sense to you—it should. We are lost in this world, but He will come and make clear every decision He makes. His light shines on us and in heaven for my brother. In this life or the next, He will give us all the answers. I know my brother and his now-perfect son are where they belong and are happy together with our Father in heaven.

We can't begin to understand why sad things happen to good people, but we just have to trust in our Lord in heaven. Even if we can never make sense of things in our human mind, we may all see the light if we can just get to heaven. I'm looking forward to being with my brother and my nephew someday when the Lord calls me home. Put your trust and love in God and you can't go wrong.

Scriptures

Lean on, trust in, *and* be confident in the Lord with all your heart *and* mind and do not rely on your own insight *or* understanding. (Proverbs 3:5)

Hear counsel, receive instruction, *and* accept correction, that you may be wise in the time to come. (Proverbs 19:20)

Blessed be the God and Father of our Lord Jesus Christ, the Father of sympathy (pity and mercy) and the God [Who is the Source] of every comfort (consolation and encouragement), (II Corinthians 1:3)

Who comforts (consoles and encourages) us in every trouble (calamity and affliction), so that we may also be able to comfort (console and encourage) those who are in any kind of trouble *or* distress, with the comfort (consolation and encouragement) with which we ourselves are comforted (consoled and encouraged) by God. (II Corinthians 1:4)

I have told you these things, so that in Me you may have [perfect] peace *and* confidence. In the world you have tribulation *and* trials *and* distress *and* frustration, but be of good cheer [take courage; be confident, certain, undaunted]! For I have overcome the world. [I have deprived it of power to harm you and have conquered it for you.] (John 16:33)

The Power of Prayer

This prayer lesson starts about thirty years ago. I felt great love, and still do, for my father. He was a good man, but he did have some faults. Pop, as I called him, was a loving-and-giving dad. Many times in my prayer life I would thank my dear Father in heaven for His grace and love in giving me a near perfect earthly father. How blessed can you be to have two fantastic fathers in your life?

The following incident started with a call to my workplace telling me to get to the hospital. I was told my dad was in deep trouble. When I arrived and saw him, he looked nine months pregnant—all swollen in the midsection. The medical staff was preparing him for emergency surgery. I had just enough time to give him my love and let him know I would be praying for him.

Doctors told us he had an aortic aneurysm and there was no time to transfer him to another hospital better set up to handle the massive bypass surgery he needed. The staff said they had never performed this type of operation, and the surgeon gave us little to no hope of Pop surviving the procedure.

The whole family was devastated. Pop was in his late fifties, and none of us were ready to give him up. They took him away, and I headed straight to the chapel. All I could do was pray. I was in tears as I said my prayers. I begged God to spare my father's life—not only was he my father, he was my best friend. I asked our heavenly Lord to let him survive and let me have my father in my world for as long as possible before he was called home.

After crying and praying for the better part of two hours, I joined my family in the waiting room. Many more hours passed. The surgeon finally walked into the room, and our hearts sank to the floor. The doctor told us Pop lived through the surgery and the next day or two would tell us more. He also told us the only thing that saved our beloved Pop was a small membrane over the exact location of the aorta where it was about to burst. The doctor also said that if the artery had let go in the operating room, Pop would not have lived.

Please think of this small membrane and where it came from. Luck? Some would say so, but not me, because by this time in my life, I had seen many prayers answered. I believe this was an act of God, and I think that was also what the doctor thought.

With six feet of plastic replacing part of his lower aorta and running down each side of his groin, Pop lived another twenty years. We enjoyed every one of those years—most filled with very good times full of love.

Later, when his health began to fail, Pop underwent several surgeries and procedures. Each time, I would pray God's will be done. I believed it was not my right to ask that Pop not suffer any more than necessary just because of my selfish desire to keep him in my life. That prayer had been answered twenty years before. I also knew that when Pop passed, we would someday be together again in peace and love, forever in our Lord's eternal reward.

The lesson learned from this story is the power of prayer when it seems there is no hope and all that we have is our God's power. With God all things are possible. If we rely on luck in troubled times, we are lost for sure.

If you believe in the power of prayer, I cannot say all things will turn out fine, but God hears our prayers and it is always His will that is done. And when He hears our prayers, many are granted—especially when they are for a good and loving reason. Pray for all things and trust in God. His power is all we must lean on. Thank you, Lord, for your grace and mercy.

Scriptures

For in You, O Lord, do I hope; You will answer, O Lord my God. (Psalm 38:15)

The Lord is near to all who call upon Him, to all who call upon Him sincerely *and* in truth. (Psalm 145:18)

For everyone who keeps on asking receives; and he who keeps on seeking finds; and to him who keeps on knocking, [the door] will be opened. (Matthew 7:8)

Up to this time you have not asked a [single] thing in My Name [as presenting all that I AM]; but now ask *and* keep on asking and you will receive, so that your joy (gladness, delight) may be full *and* complete. (John 16:24)

So, too the [Holy] Spirit comes to our aid *and* bears us up in our weakness; for we do not know what prayer to offer *nor* how to offer it worthily as we ought, but the Spirit Himself goes to meet our supplication *and* pleads in our behalf with unspeakable yearnings *and* groanings too deep for utterance. (Romans 8:26)

ADULTHOOD

Flying a Kite

A story about my grandson Dylan at the age of four or five.

This story is not about me, but I feel it is worthy of mention in my life journey. It showed me Dylan was chosen at a very young age to become a child of God. There is nothing more beautiful than the faith of a child, and Dylan showed it with his simple prayer and question. A sunny afternoon revealed the spirit of my grandson, chosen by the Lord to be a follower. Thank you, Jesus, and bless you, Dylan.

I know that God loves Dylan even more than I do. I also know that even if Dylan drifts away, our holy Shepherd will lift him up and carry him back to the flock of believers.

On a spring day, my wife and I took Dylan and his brother Jackson up to a pasture beside our barn to fly kites. Grandma was with Jackson, and I was with Dylan. We had not so much as a breeze and could not launch the kites. After about twenty minutes, Jackson and Grandma gave up and went back to the house.

Dylan was younger and more patient and wanted to try a while longer. Out of the blue, he said, "God, we sure could use some wind." I was a bit surprised to hear him say this short, but to-the-point, prayer. Dylan asked me if God heard all our prayers. I assured him that God is everywhere and hears all our thoughts and prayers. At that moment, a small wind kicked up, and we got our kite launched. It flew almost to our neighbor's property and then fell to the ground.

I am positive God wanted to show Dylan He heard his prayer. Knowing God couldn't change the weather for everyone, getting the kite up thrilled Dylan—even if it was only for a few moments.

My faith journey, like Dylan's, started at an early age. I hope Dylan remembers that sunny Sunday as I am sure that, like me, God chose Dylan while he was still very young and was already preparing a spot in heaven for my grandson. Just as a postscript, several years later on Christmas Eve, I asked Dylan whose birthday we were celebrating. He very quickly answered Jesus. Again I felt he had a connection with faith in our Lord and God.

Dylan, if you stray as I have many times, Jesus is waiting for you to come back and say, "I believe in Your love for me. I'm sorry for my wrong doings. I do still love You and want to be with You and my grandpa some day in heaven."

Scriptures

The Lord is far from the wicked, but He hears the prayer of the [consistently] righteous (the upright in right standing with Him). (Proverbs 15:29)

You will make your prayer to Him, and He will hear you, and you will pay your vows. (Job 22:27)

Listen to my prayer, O God, and hide not Yourself from my supplication! (Psalm 55:1)

Hear my cry, O God; listen to my prayer. (Psalm 61:1)

And this is the confidence (the assurance, the privilege of boldness) which we have in Him: [we are sure] that if we ask anything (make any request) according to His will (in agreement with His own plan), He listens to a*nd* hears us. (I John 5:14)

The Missing Road

Following is an exciting revelation of being spared by the Lord. I believe that my angel was supplied by God to protect me from certain death. What I am about to tell you would be almost impossible to pull off, even with a trained stuntman. This incident again proves an ultimate plan formed by the Almighty Father for the sake of my living until the time of my complete salvation.

Two friends give witness to an event that no one, including me, could believe at the time it took place. I had to stand back and admit someone, or something, was looking out for my well-being. Even my buddies agreed. I say when events such as this happen to you, give thanks and praise to the Holy Trinity. Do not try to figure them out, just accept God's love and protection and his miracles.

In my late forties, I decided to buy a used off-road motorcycle to ride with a buddy at his friend's house. We headed out on a Saturday morning. The used two-stroke had badly worn universal tires, and it was a muddy day in the woods and on the trails.

My buddy and his friend were getting a kick watching me losing control of the rear end of the bike and wiping out. After we stopped for a break, they told me to lead the way. We were about a mile out, and I am sure they just wanted to watch my spills and laugh.

I did not notice the detour we took when we started our ride because I was trying to follow and keep the bike on both wheels. Heading back, we were on a fairly straight dirt road with puddles and mud. I was keeping the bike up and started to open the throttle. In high gear, we were probably going nearly forty-five miles an hour.

All of a sudden, and I mean sudden, the road was gone! Seeing a steel beam going across the missing road, I aimed the old bike and hit the beam, with not even a chance to slow down. It seemed I was instantly thrown across a nearly thirty-foot gap that was probably the same depth.

Most likely I should have been killed, or at the very least, badly broken up. My riding buddies took a detour around the gap and met me on the other side. They were no longer laughing. Both admitted it was a bad decision to put me in the lead when I didn't know the trail. Both were utterly amazed I pulled off the crossing, and so was I.

Thanking my guardian angel, my buddy's friend took the lead, and we headed back to his house. I felt tired but lucky I had no injuries. On the way home, my buddy said someone was looking after me. I said I was thinking the same thing. A couple of weeks later, he called me and said he was riding that same path and stopped at the crossing to look at the beam I went over. He was surprised to find it bent and twisted and said it was impossible to do what I did on worn-out muddy tires.

I was not to die that day, and my Lord and angel saw to it. Maybe just luck? I don't think so—thanks be to the Lord and His saints; I still had things to do in this world.

Scriptures

For it is written, He will give His angels charge over you to guard *and* watch over you closely *and* carefully. (Luke 4:10)

I shall not die but live, and shall declare the works *and* recount the illustrious acts of the Lord. (Psalm 118:17)

And he said to Him, If You are the Son of God, throw Yourself down; for it is written, He will give His angels charge over you, and they will bear you up on their hands, lest you strike your foot against a stone. (Matthew 4:6)

He will not allow your foot to slip *or* to be moved; He Who keeps you will not slumber. (Psalm 121:3)

For He will give His angels [especial] charge over you to accompany *and* defend *and* preserve you in all your ways [of obedience and service]. (Psalm 91:11)

And you shall be secure *and* feel confident because there is hope; yes, you shall search about you, and you shall take your rest in safety. (Job 11:18)

My help comes from the Lord, Who made heaven and earth. (Psalm 121:2)

Age 7 –

Not until about age 67 did Clark know –

"If you let him live, I will give him to you."

My Brother's Lights

This incident, as told by my oldest brother, took place approximately three months before learning that my cancer had gone away. In October, my brother was on a hunting trip for elk in the southwest. While on his trip and thinking about my cancer diagnosis, my brother was saddened. He decided to ask the good Lord to have mercy on me and see to it that I would live so we could have a future together.

When he opened his eyes after praying, he saw bright, flashing lights. My brother thought it was a definite message from God that a healing would take place in my life. He was absolutely right! Although the healing may not have been at that instant, I am sure it was a sign letting him know things would be all right in time.

There were so many prayers for my recovery; who could possibly say when the exact moment of healing took place? But the lights after his prayer strengthened his faith in our Lord's power and mercy. I have thanked my brother many times for taking time on a hunting trip to think of me and say prayers on my behalf. This incident affirms my brother is also clay in our Lord's hands. I told him I pray for him daily as well.

Although the lights my brother saw on this day were not my vision, I know he would never lie to me. I believe this story as much as if it took place in my own journey. I know this incident in my brother's life strengthened his faith, and I thank my Father and Master for this.

From the time of my youth, I have held my oldest brother in high esteem—a hero in my eyes. Being ten years older than me, he taught me about the many ways of the outdoors and shooting. He always protected me and showed me love. In peace and love we live. Our love for each other is evident.

Scriptures

For in You, O Lord, do I hope; You will answer, O Lord my God. (Psalm 38:15)

Delight yourself also in the Lord, and He will give you the desires *and* secret petitions of your heart. (Psalm 37:4)

Hear my cry, O God; listen to my prayer. (Psalm 61:1)

And whatever you ask for in prayer, having faith *and* [really] believing, you will receive. (Matthew 21:22)

The Lord has heard my supplication; the Lord receives my prayer. (Psalm 6:9)

For You cause my lamp to be lighted *and* to shine; the Lord my God illumines my darkness. (Psalm 18:28)

Stage-Four Cancer and the Cure

The following story reveals just how much the Lord was molding my life. At the time, I was unhappy with my job and found that the new job I had recently taken wasn't any better. I actually asked God to end my life. That was a huge mistake. Please, don't ever say you want to die because the Lord just may answer your wish.

The journey that followed showed me just how much being alive meant to me. Even though I had asked for my life to end, our holy Father in heaven and my sweet savior Jesus walked with me the entire time and revealed the love and forgiveness that blessed my spirit.

I learned why people in extremely adverse conditions say that it was the best thing that ever happened to them. God is so merciful and full of love for us all.

Here this story begins with a dream about my father who had been gone for more than ten years. This is the most realistic dream I have ever had. We hugged, and I told him how much I had missed him. I could feel him, his presence, and the love we have for each other. He didn't speak, but I felt his love and then the dream was over. I thought about it for days.

Following the dream, and soon after I started a new job, I found a lump under my arm. I was diagnosed with stage-four cancer and was told I was in trouble. The cancer was all through me. I thought about my dream and wondered if my dad was trying to tell me that we would be together soon, or that everything would be okay. I would find out soon.

After CAT scans, biopsies, and nuclear scans, I was placed on very strong chemo to try to stop the growing weed inside my body. With God's grace I handled the chemicals pretty well. But chemo does take its toll. At the time of my first biopsy, while lying in a darkened room, I felt alone and in need of help. I prayed to Jesus to give me strength and comfort. I swear I felt a soothing presence in that room.

When I returned home, I said that only one set of footprints would show in the sand, and I was right. The *Footprints in the Sand* reflection has always been on my wall, even in the office at my shop. (*Footprints in the Sand* is included after this story.)

Before starting chemo treatments, the doctor found the cancer had spread through my body. It was on and between my ribs, under my sternum, on my liver, and spleen, and my pelvic area was full of it. It was painful. I turned to prayer and preparing for the next life, thinking this one was over. When receiving treatment, I would ask the Holy Spirit to flow with the chemicals through my body. I would also see, in my mind's eye, a small Jesus inside me gathering up cancer cells in His white robe. He would exit my body and scatter the diseased cells to the wind.

At times, darkness tried to take over my thoughts. It was a constant battle. One day, feeling sorry for myself, I wrote a list of everything I had lost in the past year and cried with each thought I listed. I showed the list to my oldest daughter and she said,

"Dad, why don't you make a list of the things you've gained in the last year?"

The next morning, I started that new list and threw the old one away. The new list was twice as long as the dark list. It included such things as friends I didn't know I had; people praying for me, some of whom I didn't even know; and becoming closer to God. And the list went on. I decided this illness was the best thing that ever happened to me. Sounds crazy, but that is how I felt even though I would still, at times, fight dark thoughts.

Four months passed, and I was due for a chemo treatment and oncologist appointment. Once again, the dark one tried to take over my thoughts. It was telling me that this was the time to end my life and get things over with. I had to fight hard for hours and turned to God in prayer for help.

I won the battle, and at the next visit, we were told the cancer was gone above the waist and what showed below the waist could be scar tissue, which turned out to be the case. Darkness had tried to take me before I found out I was cured. I learned from this that when in trouble, I need to turn to God and not give up. I believe the Lord gave me this battle to bring me closer to Him because He knew I had a job to do. That job is caring for my offspring, sharing stories to try to save as many souls as possible, and giving people hope in adversity.

My wife and I set a follow-up appointment with an oncologist at another clinic. After reviewing all the facts, he believed I had been given the wrong treatment. He was surprised the cancer went away as it had. We were told my story was shared at the clinic oncology meetings. It seems the staff knew something of a miracle had occurred. God gave me the job of bringing as many people to faith as possible—or at least trying.

Honor to the Lord with thanks and praise. I want to emphasize that, while receiving treatment at the hospital, I met many special people—a number of whom have been lost. Why the Lord decided I should be rescued would take me years to understand.

My family, especially my grandchildren, were instrumental in my recovery. Watching my grandkids play in the backyard lifted me up. Even when pain was present, grandchildren were one of the most healing things in my journey. Love lifts us up and gives us strength to go on.

I wondered for years why God spared me. Now in the late winter of life, with heart problems and lung disease, the Lord has let me know. My family helped me receive healing and now I owe it to them, if possible, to offer them spiritual healing. The Lord spared my life just for this time so I could write down my story. I am clay in God's hands. Even if I save just one soul, my time will have been well spent.

I love you all so deeply.

Footprints in the Sand
Author Unknown

The story below helps explain why, when the cancer was found, I said, "Jesus, looks like there will be only one set of footprints."

One night I had a dream. I was walking along the beach with the Lord, and across the skies flashed scenes from my life. In each scene I noticed two sets of footprints in the sand. One was mine and one was the Lord's.

When the last scene of my life appeared before me, I looked back at the footprints in the sand and, to my surprise, I noticed that many times along the path of my life, there was only one set of footprints. And I noticed it was at the lowest and saddest times in my life. I asked the Lord about it. "Lord, you said that once I decided to follow you, you would walk with me all the way. But I noticed that during the most troublesome times in my life there is only one set of foot-prints. I don't understand why you left my side when I needed you most." The Lord said, *My precious child, I never left you during your time of trial. Where you see only one set of footprints, I was carrying you.*

My Cancer Journey Daily Journal

Following are excerpts taken from my daily journal, written during my cancer journey. The decision has been made to exclude many mentions of pain and some personal family entries.

What I share are thoughts of hope and God's love and blessings during this time of spiritual and physical healing in my life. I hope and pray that you will find comfort and courage in these words, which are all exactly copied from my journal as handwritten the day they took place.

I hope some will find courage and strength in these entries. Where there is God, we have hope. Pray and stay strong.

August 1, 2005 through June 2, 2006

August 1, 2005
    New job, notice sweats and fatigue.

August 3, 2005
    Discover painless lump, right armpit.

August 31, 2005
    Prepare paper for my daughters in case I don't make it. On list, I ask my daughters to teach my grandchildren how to pray and learn the teachings of Jesus.

September 2, 2005

During a scan, I ask Jesus to lift me up and give me courage. He's there for me.

September 4, 2005

Have picnic with kids and grandkids—this picks me up. My grandson asked me if I'm sick. I just answered, "Yes, I am." He then asked, "When you stay in the little house, can my sister and me come and see you?" I gave a big smile and said, "Absolutely, anytime you want." God bless these grandchildren.

September 6, 2005

PET scan at 1:30 p.m.—painless, except for shunt, but time-consuming. Much prayer for myself, my wife, and the poor people in the Gulf Coast. The prayer helps pass the time and lifts me up.

September 9, 2005

I ask the Lord to give me a hand to stop smoking cigarettes. Just a few smokes this first day. I ask the Lord to maybe make them taste bad. I don't know how many I lit up and stomped out because they tasted like chemicals. Thank you, Jesus.

September 11, 2005

Cigs still taste like chemicals. Won't be long until I'm done with them all together.

September 12, 2005

Doctor ordered no smoking, period. I have a very low nicotine level and just went cold turkey. Thank you, Lord. Much prayer during chemo treatment. Asked Jesus and the Holy Spirit to travel with chemicals and wipe this out. I figure if He helped me to get off cigarettes, He is on my side. Started to feel positive and strong in the cancer center. The power of prayer is awesome. Thank you, Lord.

September 16, 2005

Haircut scheduled for 10:30 a.m. The hairdresser asked me if I'm angry at God. I said, "No way, He's my strength and gives me courage to fight. Without my God I'm nothing."

October 3, 2005

Hair is falling out by the handfuls. Nothing I can do about it—besides, I already told the Lord I would be willing to give up my hair and beard to be able to save one soul with my testimony. If it is His will that I survive, He has already given me so much help with everything. It feels like a given that I will survive. Just have to humble myself by losing a few things and come out on the other side a better human being.

October 6, 2005

Have to force myself to eat and drink. Still very depressed, again thinking bad things. I turned to prayer and my Bible. After a few minutes, it hits me that if I give up now, it's just like slapping Jesus in the face after everything He's done for me. I love Jesus so much, no way can I let Him down. Also, how can I ever offer testimony and help anyone if I give up now? How can I ever think of letting down all my loved ones and friends, who are praying and pulling for me? Thank you, Jesus, my prayers have been answered once again. You've given me the strength and the power to go on.

October 7, 2005

Woke up 2:00 am Friday morning and, to my surprise, hardly any pain. Is this my reward for trusting Jesus? I'd like to think so. Thank you, Lord. This has been a good lesson. If you do something to end it, or you give up a day or two too soon, sometimes relief and healing are just around the corner. Always hold on and keep praying. Maybe when I have another bad spell, I can look back on this and it will give me hope.

October 20, 2005

I've heard some say that the after-effects of chemo get worse as you receive more treatments. Thankfully I'm not seeing or feeling this. At this point I'm still looking forward from the funky week to the good week after treatments. Knowing that as the week goes on I'll feel better, which gives me strength and hope. God is with me, and I give thanks. Looking forward to granddaughter's party tomorrow evening. Sure hope I feel good enough to eat pizza.

Hard to believe she's eight years old. Can't even put into words how much I love these kids. I'm blessed.

October 23, 2005

Finished the book *Love, Medicine, and Miracles by Bernie S. Siegel, MD.* I think everyone with a serious health problem should read this. It's an older book, but it's full of advice and hope for self-healing and love.

October 28, 2005

Next week starts everything all over again. With God's mercy and grace, I'll survive all this and start over. I pray every day for guidance about how I can serve the rest of my days with testimony and praise.

November 5, 2005

Not too much exciting today. Stayed home and rested. I did get to sit outside with the grandkids and watch them play, pretty good for November. All in all, still thankful for the day. It could be so much worse, so thank you, Lord.

November 9, 2005

Try to do some extra praying today and try to figure out why I'm not picking myself up. Can't tell if it's physical or mental. It took a lot of praying, but I'm pretty sure it's the test tomorrow. I'm afraid, and that means my faith must be weak. The darkness is playing with my head; the fear is weakness and temptation. I feel the first of next week I'll pretty much know how much of a chance I have.

I have to pray and have faith in the healing of Christ. I have to ask for strength and courage in case I have other battles ahead. Also have to ask for stamina; I'm getting tired, and I think it's mental fatigue as well as physical. I want to be up and think positive tomorrow when I'm under the machine. I'll ask Jesus for one set of footprints; He'll be there for me. I have a feeling prayer will put me to sleep tonight.

November 12, 2005

Friends picked us up and took us out to dinner. We met a group of their camping neighbors, and we had a great time. Sat right across from a cancer survivor; she's been in remission for five years. It was good to talk to her and compare experiences. God keep her well.

November 14, 2005

Another uplifting, happy, spiritual day. The doctor walked in the room with a smile on her face and said, "Good news!" She sat down and pulled out charts. Liver and spleen lesions are gone, chest lesions and ribs are clean. I said, "Thank you, Lord," and the doctor smiled. Also, abdomen is normal. The only location showing involvement is in my pelvis, and now it's mild when before it was severe. All the lesions in that area are reduced by more than fifty percent. Maybe the healing moved down my body.

The first things to reduce in size that she knew of were in my neck and armpits.

I have a week and a half to write my prayer of Thanksgiving to read to the whole family on Thanksgiving Day. I have to sit and give praise and thanks. I thanked the doctor and have been thanking Jesus all day.

Just thought I'd mention about the fact I was feeling weak in my faith because I feared hearing the results of the scan. The dark one was even trying to talk me into self-harm just days before the results I spoke of. I prayed to Jesus to kick these evil thoughts out of my head and strengthen my faith. It takes prayer, but it works, and Jesus works. Thank you, my Lord Jesus, and all the people who are praying for me and who care. What a lucky and gifted person I am—what a glorious Monday.

November 15, 2005

Everyone we tell about the report says it's a miracle. What a testimony I'm going to have. Not that modern medicine didn't have a portion in this healing, but modern medicine didn't carry me test-to-test and procedure-to-procedure—my Lord Jesus did. When I felt lonely—during a biopsy, lying in a darkened room, waiting for a lab report—I asked Jesus for help, and I felt Him in the room with me.

The day after surgery—after a bone marrow biopsy—I was in much pain and had to lay under another machine. I again asked for help, and He carried me the rest of the way. Powerful medicine, and all you have to do is ask for it. I could go on and on. The smoking, with His help, stopped. The temptation to harm myself many times was ended with prayer and the strength of Jesus.

What I'm saying is trusting your doctor and the ability of modern medicine is good and necessary. But I believe that healing is a two-lane road, and a big part is faith and prayer. Jesus is there for us, and all it takes is a request. Thank you, God the Father, the Son, and the Holy Spirit.

November 17, 2005

I know I'll have help and am thanking and praising Jesus constantly. How could I have done this on my own? What a gift we have laying in front of us; all we have to do is pick it up and accept it.

November 19, 2005

Started at Psalm 145 and read to the end of Psalms. I was told Psalms 145:3–10 were for praise, and when I went there, I couldn't stop reading. What a great place to read scripture and give praise.

November 24, 2005

Thanksgiving Day and the first snowstorm of the season started last night. I know I have to venture out to get Mom later—hope the roads clear up some.

November 26, 2005

Going to church with friends tomorrow. Hope my innards don't rumble too much during the service. I'm going to pray for patience and a better mood. With the news I received, why can't I seem to keep myself up? The Lord will help me if I ask. Wish I could get off the chemicals, but that won't be for a while. With prayer, feeling good should be in my future again, God willing. I'm sick and tired of being sick and tired. I'm thankful but can't help not feeling good. Pick me up, Lord, and carry me.

November 27, 2005

Started the day going to church. Start to feel uplifted. Wife and I had a quiet and peaceful evening. I go in for chemo tomorrow. I won't be negative; I've had too many good chemo Mondays. I'll take it as it comes with the help of God.

November 28, 2005

Another good chemo day.

November 29, 2005

Rested in the morning. Feel real good today. We'll see what happens tomorrow. Like I said over and over, I have to take it one day at a time.

November 30, 2005

Graham crackers and apple sauce tastes like a mouthful of chemicals. This is a new one—always an adventure, never know what's next. Just wait and see what tomorrow brings.

December 1, 2005

Four months since I discovered the lump. In less than half that time I'll be off the chemicals and trying to decide how I want to live the rest of my life. Sure feels good saying that. I have to give credit where credit is due. Thank you, my Lord Jesus, for picking me up and carrying me the last four months. My thanks and praise. Told my wife, "How times fly when you're having fun!"

December 3, 2005

Talked to my mother today. We agree it's too bad you can't choose to live without a future of pain and loss. That's not living. You have to want to live bad enough to accept life as it is. And you have the perfect crutch to get around on in those bad times—Jesus. He will always be there for me, and He always has been. I'm so blessed to have a future with beautiful things in it and a few rocky creeks to cross, but my Lord Jesus will help me across. Life with Jesus; I'll take it and give thanks.

December 9, 2005

Very little pain today, just a few shooters. It gives me a taste of life after chemo. I continue to give thanks and praise and ask forgiveness and, of course, read scripture every day. I'm thankful and blessed.

December 11, 2005

More chemo tomorrow, and it starts all over again. Now past the halfway mark and starting on the downside—the final stretch, so to speak. I get weary of feeling bad, but I'll deal with it and feel blessed and lucky to have done so well.

December 16, 2005

Talked to my mother. She told me she fell, and some people had to lift her up. Everybody's falling; it's weird, just too much ice. By God's mercy, she received no injuries—maybe another Christmas gift. I'll say thank you, Lord. We need a warm spell to get rid of this ice. I'll include that in my prayers.

December 21, 2005

Feeling much better today. I'm thankful, a break is needed. Actually finished up some Christmas shopping and wrapped some presents. Nice just to accomplish something. I believe my prayers were heard. Not completely pain free, but a far cry from previous days.

December 22, 2005

Went into a funk this evening. I'm ashamed to say I couldn't stop weeping. It started with a movie about Jesus. I felt my love for Him and wanted to be with Him. My wife told me He's with me, and He is not ready for me to come home. She said He has plans for me, and He'll fill me in when He's ready. I know she's right; the love I have for Jesus overwhelms me at times.

December 23, 2005

I so long to be normal again, but I have a couple more months of this, and the Lord will help get me through to March. If I still drank, I think I would get drunk on my birthday, but there are better ways to celebrate. Lord, please lift me up and carry me tomorrow. I need to be held.

December 24, 2005

Christmas Eve, hard to believe it's here. Went to my daughter's house for a pig out and gift exchange at around 4:00 p.m. Got home at 8:00 p.m. We are both exhausted but had a fantastic time. We love these grandkids so much it hurts sometimes.

December 25, 2005

Christmas Day. Well, the cat got us both up before dawn. I put on a pot of vanilla-flavored coffee, and we had some cheese Danish. Kind of a tradition of ours on our Savior's birthday. We sat for a while and then opened our gifts. The highlight for me was giving Lisa a grandmother's ring. When a gift makes her cry, I know I did well. We both enjoyed ourselves. Later, we got cleaned up and went to church. Had communion with good people, good songs, and worship.

Going to take a minute and make a note: was feeling melancholic about the fact I almost didn't get to see this holiday, can't really explain the feeling. Then a voice popped in my head and told me this is the first of the rest of my holidays and to make each one better than the last. The voice had to be the Lord, because I'm not that smart. Merry Christmas, and Happy Birthday, Jesus.

December 27, 2005

First time I've had an evening out with a couple of friends in months. They pampered me and had me sitting most of the evening. Had a fantastic time. Was on the road home at 9:30 p.m. We were even talking about a clay bird shoot. I'll take my portable chair and have a blast, so to speak. No booze, just a good visit. I'm thankful.

December 28, 2005

Headed in for my chemo treatment. Found out after the blood test today that I'm anemic. They gave me a shot into my chemo shunt. The nurse says that explains the fatigue and the shortness of breath. I'm not getting enough oxygen to my body, not enough red cells to carry it. At least they're on top of things. With the good Lord's hand in this, it will all work out. I'll be tired for another month or so. What else is new? If I need a lift, I'll ask Jesus, He's always willing to lend a hand.

December 31, 2005

Went to my youngest daughter's house for wings and pizza for supper. We came home to watch a movie, and I took a nap. The kids called twice, trying to get us back over there. So we got ready and walked over. It was sure nice to bring in 2006 with our kids and grandkids. A very special New Year's Eve for both my wife and I, and we think for the kids also. Thank you, Lord.

January 1, 2006 through June 2, 2006

January 1, 2006

I don't have to go anywhere until midweek for blood tests. So I'll just rest and take it easy. Makes me feel lazy, but I can't help it. On chemo, you do what you can and when you can with no need for an explanation; it is what it is.

January 2, 2006

When you are not doing anything, you can't write about it. Let's just see what tomorrow brings.

January 5, 2006

I slept all day. Don't know how you can sleep all night and then sleep all day, but I've mastered it. Tomorrow I go in for a CT scan and a pulmonary test. At least I won't be able to sleep all morning.

January 7, 2006

Went to a country club for my wife's work party. The food was great. The night out felt good. A lady my wife works with gave me a book and a DVD—the same one she had given to her father when he had cancer. In her card, she said she prayed for me every day. It touched me deeply. What a nice gesture.

God bless her. Home by 9:30 p.m., tired but feeling blessed.

January 9, 2006

Oldest daughter is going with me for my chemo treatment on Wednesday. I'm looking forward to it. That will make the treatment fly by. I love just sitting and talking with her. I hope Jesus feels the same about me. Love is good.

January 15, 2006

Wife and I went to church this morning. It feels good to sit with friends and her, and pray and worship.

January 16, 2006

I went outside and stood in the sun. Youngest daughter's oldest son came out for a visit. Felt like October again. Great spending time with him—what a good, loving five-year-old. I hope and pray he never changes. I consider these times together a gift to me. I am a wealthy man to be able to have so much love in my life. Thank you, Lord, for all those I love and all those who love me. And most importantly, Lord, thank You for Your love for all of us.

January 28, 2006

The chemicals hit today. Slight depression, pain, and impatience. Highs and lows all day. Granddaughter helps to pick me up. She gave me a glass star that she held when praying for me. The power of children's love is like nothing else. God bless her. I will get through the day, and tomorrow will be better. Dear Lord, give me courage and strength.

February 7, 2006

It's the hospital tomorrow for a fresh-new batch of chemicals. After that, just one more chemo scheduled. With God's grace, all the cancer cells will be gone.

February 8, 2006

Rested a little in the morning then got cleaned up and onto chemo treatment. Everything went well. Red-cell count going up, and white cells are holding their own. I did much praying when the chemicals were going in. Seem to always have a nice conversation with people and find it an uplifting experience. I forgot to mention, I asked the doctor about the moderate to severe pain in pelvic area; she agrees it's the medicine attacking tumor growth. Again, good news, that's what I'm praying for. Another rewarding treatment day. Thank You, Lord, my prayers are being granted.

February 13, 2006

Wanted to go to the bank and store today. That's not going to happen. Maybe tomorrow will be better. Just go with the flow and pray for my Savior's help. He's always there for me. He's my rock and my strength.

February 16, 2006

I'm going to declare this treatment is one of the top two worst chemo I've had. That tells me the last one won't be as bad. With God's grace, I'm almost finished with the chemicals.

February 25, 2006

Nice sunny February day. Just warm enough for me to be able to sit outside and pray in the sun. Don't know why I always feel closer to God outside, but I've always been that way. Hard to believe this could become, with God's mercy, my last chemo treatment. Like a dream, I'm thinking about getting strong enough to ride my cycle. Maybe take a hike in the woods, do some chores, shoot a couple of guns, maybe do some work and earn some money. God's will be done. All this will be possible. I continue to pray and trust in the Lord.

February 27, 2006

It seems several days after chemo, I'm on overload. I believe the chemical is maxed out, and it's all I can handle on these days. I want no problems, I won't talk money, and I don't want to talk on the phone. I don't want company. I just want to put up with how I feel all by myself. This, thankfully, will only last a day or two. I don't plan this, and I can't help it. That's just how it is. I turned to prayer and silence to make it through the day. All this will pass, and things will get better.

March 3, 2006

Feeling a bit more up today. Did some chores. The pain seems to be more manageable. A good sign toward evening, I was cracking jokes and teasing my wife. She even said, "You must be feeling better."

March 4, 2006

Beautiful day. Decided to do a few chores and get a little laundry done over at the farm. I came home, sat in the sun, and prayed. Then the grand-kids came out. My five-year-old grandson came over and put his arms around me and said, "I love you grandpa." That's what living is all about. The visit didn't last long though—my daughter caught them running through the dog's poopy area. They were called inside. See you, kids!

March 9, 2006

Yesterday the doctor asked me to start walk-ing twenty minutes a day. So I chose a time when it wasn't raining, and part way it felt like my hips were giving out. I slowed down but continued, and the pain started to subside. I like the way it made me feel.

March 10, 2006

Much less pain today. Took my twenty-minute walk. Again, hips felt like they were giving out, but as I kept walking, the pain eased. Legs felt good the rest of the day. The chemicals seem to be wearing off. No more chemo until March 23. Maybe seeing how it feels to be off the chemo will renew my desire to fight some more.

March 11, 2006

Nice easy morning. Feeling up and ready to go.

March 12, 2006

We went to church, but we left a little before the service ended. Pains in my legs, and service was long. A little sore today, but not as bad as anticipated. The chemicals are wearing off. Even took my walk in the afternoon. I helped with supper and dishes, but not much else. All in all, not a bad day, and I give thanks. Will see what the first of the week brings.

March 16, 2006

Keeping up with my twenty-minute walks. Today, hips seem to loosen up easier. Went just a little further. No major pain today. Hope this is an indication of days to come. Maybe a taste of what I'm continuing to fight for.

March 17, 2006

Still feel good enough to head over to the farm and do some laundry. Took my walk while the dryer is running. Did some praying and read some New Testament. It's a beautiful day with sunshine and lots of blue skies. Another taste of what life is worth fighting for. I think the good Lord is maybe trying to send me some help.

March 23, 2006

Arrived at the hospital at 7:45 a.m. for a scan. Prayer helped me lay still for the time the exam takes. After the scan was completed, I met my wife at the oncologist office. The doctor walked in and said the scan shows nothing, then she said the word every cancer fighter longs to here—remission!

My wife cried, and I could hardly believe it. I've been down the last couple of weeks, thinking of the CAT scan still showing cancer in my pelvis. Guess what—scar tissue! I mentioned to Lisa a day or two ago that I wondered if it was all scar tissue. I prayed for just that outcome. Never give up hope; you just never know what the good Lord has in store. This last week or two was just God giving me one last hurdle, and I made it.

There are still things to be done. My doctor wants me to see a lymphoma specialist and have him review all my files, just to see if he thinks any follow up is in order. My own personal follow up is prayer. In the afternoon, when all alone, I started to cry. I went down on my knees in the kitchen, folded my hands above me on the counter, and gave thanks and praise to the Lord. Not only am I now in remission, but Jesus was with me for every beat back of temptation, for every procedure, for every needle punch—with every pain, He was my foundation and strength.

From the day I heard about my illness, there has been only one set of footprints in the sand. I asked Him to carry me, and my Shepherd did so. A coworker of my wife stated, "Now he has his testimony." I pray for guidance and direction as to what to do with my new life. And I know that wisdom will be granted. And I do have a living testimony: to God's grace and mercy.

March 27, 2006

Got to hang out with the grandkids in the backyard late afternoon. That was fun. Always something to be thankful for. The oncologist at the clinic was a fine young doctor. Very intelligent, and kind. He says the slides of my biopsy will be examined by his pathologist, and my case will be brought up in a meeting—sounds important! The doctor says the cell that was finally determined doesn't act like my case. He agrees with my doctor that the pain has been nerve damage, and most of it will heal.

April 15, 2006

Looking forward to Easter and going to church in the morning. Hope I feel good and able. I am feeling little improvements. Again, I live day-by-day, keep my faith, and pray for strength.

April 16, 2006

A beautiful Easter Sunday. We went to church, and later, my granddaughter brought over a small Easter basket. All in all, a wonderful Easter.

May 18, 2006

My strength is continuing to come back. It's a slow process, but I'll take it. I'm good for approximately three hours of labor, and I also seem to recoup quicker than in the past months. I try to do something every day to rebuild muscle.

June 2, 2006

Thought it time for an update. It seems my strength is returning, and I'm good for several hours of labor. This part of my journey is over. My life starts again. I give thanks and praise to God and admit this was all a blessing that brought me closer to my Lord.

THE CLAY IS CRACKING

Heart Failure Cures Sin and Shame

I am not proud to share this part of my journey, but I think it may help some by showing how far God goes to bring us back to a full relationship. I detested this time in my life and will never go back. This account shows how the power of darkness can take over the flesh.

I thought that looking at X-rated pictures on the computer was okay. After all, the women were not live females, just pictures. And then I read the Savior's words in the New Testament, that even the thought of adultery was a sin. I realized what I was watching on the computer was adultery. That got me feeling guilty. The godly side of me asked for help to quit these actions and thoughts. I prayed to Jesus for forgiveness and to give me strength to stop.

On several occasions, I would read a title to a clip which talked filthy about Jesus. This would shock me, and I would turn the computer off. Sometimes this would last only a couple days and then I would start again.

How can anyone who is saved from cancer enter into this sin? I began to feel that my faith wasn't strong enough for me to end my shame. I again asked the Lord to rescue me. It took my Lord drastic measures to bring me to redemption, once again showing me He would not give up on my eternal spirit.

Jesus knew something had to happen. I went into heart failure, the closest I have ever been to knowing I was going to die. But He knew I wouldn't, and it rekindled a great faith inside me.

Being so close to death with so many sins shocked me. I asked forgiveness and renewed my faith. I've not looked at anything filthy since, and I have no desire to do so. I'm thankful for the close call. Sometimes God will use a dark time to pluck you out of a sinful period and bring you back closer than ever to His love and redemption.

I was not going to tell this story because of my shame. I decided though that this, and the next journey would show the length and power our mighty Lord will take to save us from our sinful lives. I'm thankful to God, and this truth brought me out of the life of sin and into a relationship of the spirit shared with the King of Hosts—praise and thanks.

Jesus knew I still had work to do, and that's why I've been spared over and over again in my life—to share my shame and recovery with those of you reading my stories. Following is another example of His grace and forgiveness.

While in the hospital, I had to undergo a heart catheterization. Lying on the table with a camera in my heart, I prayed to the Lord and asked Him to spare me from open-heart surgery. I told Jesus that I would not allow myself to be opened up and put on a breathing machine. I would take my chances and depend on His decision.

In my prayer, I used words from our Savior in the New Testament, saying, "Ask and it will be answered, knock and the door will be opened." I was praying the physician would find no blockages and that no further action would be needed.

Within five minutes, the doctor said the procedure was over, and no new blockages had been found. In fact, two older stints were blocked completely, but my body had grown new vessels around them. They were open now and required no further treatment.

Talk about prayers being answered! The doctor's words were almost exactly what I had asked for in prayer. My father had blockages, and also my sister. And I had two blockages repaired with stints about ten years prior. Yet now everything was clear. I believe in the power of prayer, and the Lord working in our lives.

Thank you, Jesus, with all my heart.

Scriptures

In Him we have redemption (deliverance and salvation) through His blood, the remission (forgiveness) of our offenses (shortcomings and trespasses), in accordance with the riches *and* the generosity of His gracious favor, (Ephesians 1:7)

I acknowledged my sin to You, and my iniquity I did not hide. I said, I will confess my transgressions to the Lord [continually unfolding the past till all is told]—then You [instantly] forgave me the guilt *and* iniquity of my sin. Selah [pause and calmly think of that]! (Psalm 32:5)

And they will no more teach each man his neighbor and each man his brother, saying, Know the Lord, for they will all know Me [recognize, understand, and be acquainted with Me], from the least of them to the greatest, says the Lord. For I will forgive their iniquity, and I will [seriously] remember their sin no more. (Jeremiah 31:34)

For My eyes are on all their ways; they are not hidden from My face, neither is their iniquity concealed from My eyes. (Jeremiah 16:17)

Let us all come forward *and* draw near with true (honest and sincere) hearts in unqualified assurance *and* absolute conviction engendered by faith (by that leaning of the entire human personality on God in absolute trust and confidence in His power, wisdom, and goodness), having our hearts sprinkled *and* purified from a guilty (evil) conscience and our bodies cleansed with pure water. (Hebrews 10:22)

I [the Lord] will instruct you and teach you in the way you should go; I will counsel you with My eye upon you. (Psalm 32:8)

Fishing in the Hospital

This story tells of a dream in which the Lord reveals to me His mercy and plans for my future. If not for a phone call, I could have just accepted the dream as a pleasant story in my sleep. However, a call from my daughter confirmed that it was a message from the Heavenly Father of hope for times to come, including fishing and spending time with my grandchildren in the great and beautiful outdoors.

If we open our minds and accept His messages, we can gather hope of healing and of God's mercy in our times of adversity. Hope is needed for healing in all things. When we know hope comes from Christ Jesus, it removes any thoughts of darkness and sheds light on the days ahead. I give praise and thanks to the masterful molder of my life.

In the hospital, with heart failure, I had a peaceful dream in which I wore no portable oxygen tank and walked around a beautiful pond. I looked down at the shore in the shallow water, and fish looked up at me. I could see them breathing underwater. The dream was so relaxing and peaceful.

In the morning, it came to me that God was telling me I would pull through this trial and enjoy peaceful days and the outdoors. I was filled with hope for the future and thanked the Master for His revelation. My Father in heaven was also telling me that He forgave my sins and still considered me His child. Again, He was molding me into His masterpiece.

Following is what sets this story in stone. On my second day home from the hospital, my youngest daughter called out of the clear blue. She told me that she had been talking with her ex-husband about my health, and he invited me to go fishing at his family's pond, just ten minutes from our house, anytime I wanted.

How is this possible other than through the grace of God? Again, the Lord was welcoming me back to His flock and renewing my faith, hope, and love. Praise and thanks to the Holy of Holiest for His undying grace.

Scriptures

And all were beside them-
selves with amazement and were
puzzled *and* bewildered, saying
one to another, What can this
mean? (Acts 2:12)

And they said to him, We
have dreamed dreams, and there
is no one to interpret them. And
Joseph said to them, Do not
interpretations belong to God?
Tell me [your dreams], I pray
you. (Genesis 40:8)

And He said, Hear now
My words: If there is a prophet
among you, I the Lord make
Myself known to him in a vision
and speak to him in a dream.
(Numbers 12:6)

These you may eat of all
that are in the waters: whatever
has fins and scales in the waters,
in the seas, and in the rivers, these
you may eat; (Leviticus 11:9)

Win-Win at the Hospital

This next event has had the most profound impact on my faith more than all the others combined.

Christ Jesus's love was revealed, not in my sleep, but in my mind's vision. Even in a very troubling time, He gave me courage, strength, and peace of mind to face anything life threw my way. Knowing He was holding me up in His clay-covered hands gave me a feeling of protection I had never experienced at this level. Finding at this time of unknowing that I had no fear of life or death was a rewarding revelation. Thank you, Lord Jesus, for your love and protection and for helping me to know you are with me at all times. My peace has been found; I am free.

I have been suffering from lung disease and heart problems for months now. The pulmonary doctor started me on steroids, not the best medicine, but he thought it necessary. During the month of May, I started downhill; I did much praying for healing, but it seemed my prayers were not being answered. I continued to grow weaker and weaker until just standing seemed impossible. I believed the end of my life was near. Everyone said I was the color of clay, and I knew trouble was imminent.

Toward the end of May, I got on my knees and cried out to the Lord, asking for help. I told Him that I was too weak even to continue my stories. I cried and told God I wanted strength to finish my writing and wanted more time with my grandchildren to finish my job here on earth.

The next day, I called the pulmonary doctor to let him know how weak my body was growing. The doctor sent me to the hospital emergency room. It was there they discovered it wasn't my lungs that wouldn't take in oxygen; I was bleeding internally and was extremely low on blood. I was admitted and given two blood transfusions. Feeling strength coming back, I now faced tests to discover where the bleed was located.

Praying that night, I saw my savior Jesus in my mind's eye. He put His arms around me and said He would always be with me and that He loved me. I have never felt that kind of love before. It was over-whelming, unlike anything I have ever felt. I started weeping. Jesus stepped back and patted my shoulder. He did not want me to weaken myself with crying. This love cannot be described; there is nothing comparable.

When this visit with Jesus was over, it came to me that I was in a win-win time in my life. If they found the bleed and fixed it, I would gain strength and continue on. If I passed, I would feel that love from Jesus for all eternity.

My fear left me because, either way, I couldn't lose. I won with the Lord and no longer feared death. Jesus gave me a small taste of heaven that most people don't experience, so you will have to take my word: don't pass up Jesus and don't pass up heaven. You cannot lose!

I still faced testing, but they found the bleed and fixed it so there is no more leakage. According to the blood test, my body was making blood. I don't know why I deserved this treatment from God, but I believe in the power of prayer, and He knows I'm going to share this story.

Again, I was the color of clay, and the Lord had me in His hands, molding my life. I was brought back to the living to finish the job the Lord wants me to do: save souls who will someday share with me the presence of God in heaven. Praise and thanks to the Almighty.

Scriptures

Therefore, we do not become discouraged (utterly spiritless, exhausted, and wearied out through fear). Though our outer man is [progressively] decaying *and* wasting away, yet our inner self is being [progressively] renewed day after day. (II Corinthians 4:16)

The person who has My commands and keeps them is the one who [really] loves Me; and whoever [really] loves Me will be loved by My Father, and I [too] will love him and will show (reveal, manifest) Myself to him. [I will let Myself be clearly seen by him and make Myself real to him.] (John 14:21)

[Oh, your perversity!] You turn things upside down! Shall the potter be considered of no more account than the clay? Shall the thing that is made say of its maker, He did not make me; or the thing that is formed, say of him who formed it, He has no understanding? (Isaiah 29:16)

And afterward I will pour out My Spirit upon all flesh; and your sons and your daughters shall prophesy, your old men shall dream dreams, your young men shall see visions. (Joel 2:28)

And He said, Hear now My words: If there is a prophet among you, I the Lord make Myself known to him in a vision and speak to him in a dream. (Numbers 12:6)

If any of you is deficient in wisdom, let him ask of the giving God [Who gives] to everyone liberally *and* ungrudgingly, without reproaching, *or* faultfinding, and it will be given him. (James 1:5)

[Besides this evidence] it was also established *and* plainly endorsed by God, Who showed His approval of it by signs and wonders and various miraculous manifestations of [His] power and by imparting the gifts of the Holy Spirit [to the believers] according to His own will. (Hebrews 2:4)

And the grace (unmerited favor and blessing) of our Lord [actually] flowed out superabundantly *and* beyond measure for me, accompanied by faith and love that are [to be realized] in Christ Jesus. (I Timothy 1:14)

Win-Win Again

Another trip to the emergency room with heart problems. I'm admitted and stayed nine days. The only thing different is the near-death heart stoppages, but with no fear. What a powerful feeling, to be looking at possible death and not fear it.

I know you may think this is an exaggeration, but you'll have to take my word for the power the Savior has on our lives. With God there is nothing we can't overcome.

Read now about the many tests, the final outcome of this trial, and how winning again gives me great hope for a future filled with family, love, and the telling of my story of the glory of our Lord Christ Jesus.

Here we go again. My wife is visiting with the neighbors and I enter into a fib. Heart rate went up to 250 and then dropped. When she gets home, it's off to the hospital. They cannot get my heart rate under control. I'm admitted and it all begins—tests, doctors, needles, and no sleep.

Almost all the family was with me at the hospital on the second night of my stay when my heart stopped completely in front of everyone; what a weird feeling. I think it was worse for my loved ones.

That night, while reading a book, a bizarre feeling took over. I thought maybe I was having a stroke. When I came out of it, my room was filled with people giving orders and performing their different tasks. I came to find out my heart stopped, and the people in my room were the rapid response team. I never heard the alarm on my monitor or the call for the rapid response team. This was the longest stoppage I had experienced, and that night it stopped between ten and twelve times. Needless to say, no sleep was to be had that night. My wife, who was with me, also had a very long night.

Again, my body was turned over to Jesus, and I prayed that His will be done. I asked again that my life be spared to finish my stories and spend more time with my family to win them over to the cross of Jesus. I figured He had a choice—was it a good time to take me home? But yet again, I was given life. During every procedure after that night, Jesus was with me and I felt little fear. The next day, a temporary defibrillator and pacemaker were installed. The doctors tried to shock my ticker into a regular heartbeat, but it did not work.

More procedures were on the way. What a rollercoaster of a ride. Ultrasound, X-rays, CT scan, needles, and more tests. A tube was placed down to my stomach again to make sure there was no bleeding so that I could go back on blood thinners. Then it was down the throat again to check out the back of my heart for blood clots. A permanent pacemaker with defibrillator was installed and then I was given a big shock which put my heart back in rhythm after ten days.

Through every procedure, Jesus was holding me in His loving hands, and I had little fear. This was, again, still a win-win. The whole experience gives me the message that the Lord Father, Son, and Holy Spirit wants my testimony written down for the salvation of as many souls as I can help get to heaven. And when it's finished, maybe I will get to see the winners in heaven. How can I lose with God? Win-win again. All praise and thanks to a loving and merciful God.

Some say I must be off my rocker to thank a God who would make me suffer so much. Again I repeat, we are clay in God's hands and my whole life has been molded to be right here where I am ready to face life and be with my family. I am also ready to face the end of life to be in heaven in the presence of God for all eternity. It's win-win any way you look at it. I am blessed.

Scriptures

I have been crucified with Christ [in Him I have shared His crucifixion]; it is no longer I who live, but Christ (the Messiah) lives in me; and the life I now live in the body I live by faith in (by adherence to and reliance on and complete trust in) the Son of God, Who loved me and gave Himself up for me. (Galatians 2:20)

Peace I leave with you; My [own] peace I now give *and* bequeath to you. Not as the world gives do I give to you. Do not let your hearts be troubled, neither let them be afraid. [Stop allowing yourselves to be agitated and disturbed; and do not permit yourselves to be fearful and intimidated and cowardly and unsettled.] (John 14:27)

May the God of your hope so fill you with all joy and peace in believing [through the experience of your faith] that by the power of the Holy Spirit you may

abound *and* be overflowing (bub-
bling over) with hope. (Romans
15:13)

After these things, the word
of the Lord came to Abram in a
vision, saying, Fear not, Abram,
I am your Shield, your abun-
dant compensation, *and* your
reward shall be exceedingly great.
(Genesis 15:1)

For the law of the Spirit of
life [which is] in Christ Jesus [the
law of our new being] has freed
me from the law of sin and death.
(Romans 8:2)

My flesh and my heart may
fail, but God is the Rock *and*
firm Strength of my heart and my
Portion forever. (Psalm 73:26)

The Lord is on my side; I
will not fear. What can man do
to me? (Psalm 118:6)

A Brother's Lesson

I wanted to tell my oldest brother that I did not fear death because of my relationship with my heavenly Father. I was ready to face my God. When I tried to talk to my brother about this, I learned an important lesson. I came to understand that everyone copes differently with death and the loss of a loved one.

My brother loved and supported me but wasn't ready to talk about my death and what that loss would mean to him. What I want my brother and loved ones to know is that I do not fear death. I also want to convey my total lack of fear of all the procedures and heart-stopping experiences I encountered.

I want to tell all those I love that when death is no longer feared, the love of God is worth looking forward to. But this life on earth is good, and in my prayers, I am still asking for the love of family and the enjoyment of God's creation.

I want those that I love to understand I am a man of the flesh and want to live as long as God wills. Leaving a loving family to grieve and hurt at my loss is not an easy thought. But I tell all that I guarantee where I'll be going, and it's not a place of health problems and pain, but of eternal love and peace in God's presence.

So if these words are being read after my passing, please be happy for me and find your faith in Jesus so we can share the blessings of eternal love. And from everything I have studied, I believe the faithful departed are able to watch over their loved ones from heaven and pray for them.

The lesson to my brother is, even if I precede him in death, I'll always love him, even if it is from above, and the same is expected from him. Go in peace and have the love of our savior Jesus Christ now and forever.

The Outcome and Healing

I am giving thanks that I'm still around to write about God's healing in my life. With battery-operated heartbeat control and a few different prescriptions, I returned home with renewed strength and stamina after my win-win-again experience. I've not felt this way in a couple years, and I do give credit to modern medicine, but ultimately, it was the Lord who brought me back from the edge of my earthly time.

I knew in the hospital that I'd be coming home. If the Lord wanted to call me home, He would have done it when my heart was stopping, and I underwent all the procedures.

Of course I can't predict any future problems with my health right now, but I know as well as anyone that someday God will call me home, and of that, I have no fear. I am positive He is giving me this remaining time to let everybody know of His healing grace and what He can do for us all if we let Him.

At the time of this writing, my strength is at a point that I know I'll be spending time with my family at gatherings and enjoying time outdoors. No one could ask for more. I feel the Lord's healing and rewards are now on my plate, and I'll take every minute available to me and be most thankful until the end of my time.

As I hope you can see, my whole life has been molded for this very time. Knowing I'm blessed by our Maker's plan and He resides in my spirit, again I have to state there is no fear of living or death. What a great feeling of freedom and peace to be blessed with. Only our savior, Jesus, is responsible for this beautiful masterpiece of a plan. How is it possible to thank Him enough?

Looking forward to seeing you in this world or the next. Peace and love be with your spirits.

CLAY IN GOD'S HANDS

GOD'S PLEASURE
REVEALED

Many times, things that happen in our lives which can't be explained turn out to be spiritual. I am graced over and over again with the love God feels and the pleasure He receives from my prayers and devotions. Thanks can never be enough to show how I feel toward the Lord who gives me so much mercy and grace and is always present in my life.

Look for God in your life. Open your minds and hearts and He will be there for you in all your thoughts and all that happens in your world. All praise and thanks to the center of our lives, Jesus Christ, our almighty savior.

As most Christians know, we are not to talk about our fasting—especially to boast about it. But this revelation from my Holy Father is not boasting, and I think the story should be told. This is another wonder that can't be explained and helps confirm my faith in a spiritual God who loves and lives in us and, at times, reveals Himself to us in wondrous ways.

About three weeks into Lent, after giving up a favorite food that I would eat every day, I was watching my favorite evangelist on television. He said when we fast, God will reward us for our sacrifices. The thought hit me the wrong way. I immediately told God that my fast wasn't for rewards, but to thank Him for all He has done for me, and I wanted nothing in return but His love.

This prayer must have pleased Him. Suddenly, the whole room filled with a scent that could not be explained. It was the sweetest smell I have ever encountered—almost like cotton candy but even sweeter. It lasted a few short minutes and was gone. The next morning, even though the scent hadn't smelled like perfume, I asked my wife if she had spilled any of her scents, or if our cat may have done so. She said she had gone straight to bed and nothing had been spilled. When in a spiritual relationship with God and something can't be explained, it comes to mind that it is God's pleasure revealed—in this instance, with the sweetest odor I have ever enjoyed, possibly the scent of heaven itself.

Again this story is not to boast, but to prove that when we let the Holy Spirit live in us, He will reveal Himself in ways not explainable. How wonderful it is to be shown God' pleasure in answer to a prayer. All thanks, praise, and love to my perfect Lord who bestows and shares His love on us.

Scriptures

Then [Ezra] told them, Go your way, eat the fat, drink the sweet drink, and send portions to him for whom nothing is prepared; for this day is holy to our Lord. And be not grieved *and* depressed, for the joy of the Lord is your strength *and* stronghold. (Nehemiah 8:10)

In this way [our] witnessing concerning Christ (the Messiah) was so confirmed *and* established *and* made sure in you. (I Corinthians 1:6)

Then the word of the Lord came to me [Jeremiah], saying, (Jeremiah 1:4)

The person who has My commands and keeps them is the one who [really] loves Me; and whoever [really] loves Me will be loved by My Father, and I [too] will love him and will show (reveal, manifest) Myself to him. [I will let Myself be clearly seen by him and make Myself real to him.] (John 14:21)

THOUGHTS

Fact is, we're all clay in God's hands. If we seek faith in a relationship with the Almighty, He will form and mold us to be worthy at the end of our lives. The Lord spared me through many close calls and trials, not only to disclose my stories, but to form me into a more perfect spirit worthy to be in His presence for all eternity.

My goal with these stories is to hope that some may understand how it is possible to slip away and be brought back through our shepherd, Jesus Christ, as many times as needed. At times during my many trials, I was told my skin was the color of clay. That's exactly what I was—clay being molded and formed into who God wanted me to be prior to my passing.

Please, I ask and pray for you, let our master artist in heaven mold you into a sculpture worthy of eternity with Him in paradise. When you turn yourself over to the Holy Trinity, you will feel free of fear, love more deeply than you ever have, and experience unexplained peace in your life. How any person could pass up these gifts, I don't understand.

Please let Jesus know you want Him to live in you, through His Holy Spirit. Lean on Jesus when you have earthly trials, and you will feel Him holding you up in His clay-covered hands. He will give you strength, courage, and His perfect love.

How great is our Lord who gives us hope for this world and the next! All thanks, praise, and love be given to our holiest of Holy Creator.

SIMPLE STEPS TO REDEMPTION

In your mind's eye, or out loud, God will hear you. Pray that you accept Jesus Christ as your savior, and believe He died for our sins so that they may be forgiven. And He was raised from the grave and overcame death by the power of His Father in heaven.

Tell Jesus you accept Him in your heart. Tell Him you are sorry for your sins and ask for His forgiveness.

These simple steps are called being born again. Believe and talk to Jesus like a friend and He will give you the gift of the Holy Spirit. The Holy Spirit will give you peace, courage, and strength to get through this short trial we all share in this life so we may enjoy eternity with all the faithful departed and our wonderful God in heaven. It is that easy! Please don't miss out. Let me greet you at the gates of paradise.

ABOUT THE AUTHOR

D. R. Fogle was born and raised in Canton, Ohio. He was a husband, father of two grown daughters, grandfather of six, and great-grandfather of one. As a cancer survivor, Mr. Fogle valued his faith and family as essential healing attributes while navigating life's many journeys and adventures.

Within *Clay in God's Hands*, Mr. Fogle shared personal short stories based on the empowerment of faith and love of God. When he was not spending time with his wife of forty-five years, Lisa, he enjoyed journal writing and participating in outdoor activities. *Clay in God's Hands* was Mr. Fogle's first book.

CPSIA information can be obtained
at www.ICGtesting.com
Printed in the USA
BVHW082103190722
642493BV00003B/348

9 781638 852476